Dr. V, Thank you for
inviting me to Tohidu.
Thank you for what you do!

David Rose
2016

Some Wounds Don't Bleed

(Original poetry by a Vietnam War Veteran undergoing
PTSD therapy with the Veterans Administration)

Written by: David Rose

Version 5

Foreword

If you, as I have, believed that post-traumatic stress disorder (PTSD) is a condition of recent vintage, we were both wrong. One of the challenges of an evolving language is that as new information is added about an existing condition, the naming of that condition also evolves. As a result, it may be perceived as defining something new. So it appears to have been with PTSD.

PTSD and its initializing *is* relatively new; it became part of the English vocabulary in the early 1980s. "The diagnosis of *post-traumatic stress disorder (PTSD)* emerged from the . . . American Psychiatric Association's (1980) manual of mental disorders, the *Diagnostic and Statistical Manual of Mental Disorders*, third edition" (Figley, 1985, p. xix). But, according to Figley, this diagnosis is simply the current version of a set of symptoms that physicians and psychiatrists have known about and studied for at least the past two centuries. Horwitz (2015), for example, reports that Civil War soldiers frequently suffered from the PTSD-equivalent—but that the condition was covered up because having it reflected negatively on the former soldier. Most recently, Pratap Chatterjee (215) reported a new concern about PTSD. The title of his article, "A Chilling New Post-traumatic Stress Disorder: Why Drone Pilots Are Quitting in Record Numbers," clearly states the problem.

Partially as a result of the trauma associated with the unpopular Vietnam war and our desire to address that distress, the psychiatric community coined as the new diagnostic term *post-traumatic stress disorder*, thereby replacing the previously used *post-traumatic neurosis*. PTSD—although not restricted to the trauma of war and military engagement—has become an increasingly popular diagnosis for the challenging conditions suffered by a large number of soldiers returning from the Vietnam War. Consequently, the term has become associated primarily with the trauma of war (Figley, 1985).

One of my reasons for briefly addressing the history of PTSD to point out that the condition always has had and continues to have mentally destabilizing effects that society only recently has been willing to address. My other reason is a personal one: to introduce the hero of this book, my colleague and friend, David Rose.

I first met David when he arrived in my high-school biology class in the mid 1960s, in Orlando, Florida. For reasons that we may never know, we established a friendship that has endured for decades. We were never close, but we stayed in touch. After subsequent positions in Texas, Pennsylvania, and Michigan, I moved to Chattanooga—and discovered that David had settled there as well. After a number of various and very successful but also very different careers, David spent summers working as a park ranger in Yosemite National Park. He spent winters in Chattanooga, where he continued several professional challenges.

David and I reconnected, mostly over lunch, where we brought each other up to date about our lives. It seemed natural, then, when David shared several of his poems about his experience in Vietnam. At that time, I was not aware that David spent more than forty years trying to forget what he experienced in Vietnam. Finally he could no longer keep himself busy enough to avoid his traumatic memories but he had become incredibly successful at hiding it. David tells his story in a recent article entitled "Some wounds Don't Bleed: An Examination of Unresolved

Trauma in Vietnam Veterans and Its Ethical Implications Through the Lens of One Man's Story and Beyond" (Spence, Rose, & Tucker, 2014, pp. 140-157).

Over the years, David's attempts to find help were minimized to a point where he felt that there was no hope, no way out. And then—quite by accident—he discovered poetry to be a highly therapeutic treatment of his PTSD. In the book you are holding, you will experience, through David's poetry, just how traumatic his experiences were, and you will feel the wrenching agony and realizations of a form of life-and-death situation that few of us are required to endure.

David tells me that he initially began writing poems for himself and his therapist. As the therapeutic impact of his poetry came to light, however, he decided to share them with a wider audience. He compiled his poetry into a book and he has initiated a blog to share additional poems. He also has created an online forum to discuss PTSD issues with individuals around the world: http://davidroseptsdforum.com.

By reading David's words expressed as poetry, I have become aware of the depths to which our fighting heroes descend into their psyches. They have no prior knowledge about how to cope with the resulting mental trauma, no anticipatory set of the experiences on which to rely for help. Everyone is different, of course, and some of us experience a very different life from that described in these pages. However, even if we are not engaged in combat on the front lines, life may present us with situations that are just as insurmountable as those that David expresses in his poetry.

In his book *On Killing*, Lt. Col. Dave Grossman (1996) states that "the long-term legacy of the Vietnam War upon American society is not just hundreds of thousands of troubled veterans, it is also hundreds of thousands of troubled marriages impacting women, children, and future generations (p. 291). There is a nexus of events and causation linking the death of enemy soldiers and the spittle of war protesters with a patter of suicide, homelessness, mental illness and divorce that will ripple through the United States for generations to come (p. 290). It may indeed be necessary to engage in a war, but we must begin to understand the potential long-term price of such endeavors" (p. 291).

I believe that anyone who reads David's vividly expressed thoughts will gain a greater appreciation for some of the more frightening effects of warfare on the human psyche and will be encouraged by the fact that such experiences can be dealt with by one of a number types of therapeutic intervention, including poetry.

References

American Psychiatric Association. (1980). The diagnostic and statistical manual of mental disorders (3rd ed.). Washington, DC: American Psychiatric Association.

Chatterjee, P. (2015). A chilling new post-traumatic stress disorder: Why drone pilots are quitting in record numbers. http://www.salon.com/2015/03/06/a_chilling_new_post_traumatic_stress_disorder_why_drone_pilots_are_quitting_in_record_numbers_partner/.

Figley C. R. [Ed.]. (1985). *Trauma and its wake: Volume I: The study and treatment of post-traumatic stress disorder.* Bristol, PA: Brunner/Mazel.

Grossman, D. (1996). *On killing: The psychological cost of learning to kill in war and society.* Boston, MA: Little, Brown and Company.

Horwitz, T. (2015). Did Civil War soldiers have PTSD? http://www.smithsonianmag.com/history/ptsd-civil-wars-hidden-legacy-180953652/?no-ist.

Spence, M., Rose, D., & Tucker J. A. (2014). Some wounds don't bleed: An examination of unresolved trauma in Vietnam veterans and its ethical implications through the lens of one man's story and beyond. *Ethical Human Psychology and Psychiatry,* 16: 3, pp. 140-157.

James A. Tucker, Ph.D.

McKee Chair of Excellence in Learning

University of Tennessee at Chattanooga

Preface

The following is a collection of original poetry that was written from the heart of a 65 year old Vietnam War Veteran who is in Post Traumatic Stress Disorder (PTSD) therapy with the Veterans Administration.

The purpose of this book is to help educate interested persons about the mindset of a PTSD patient and to hopefully create a connection to other PTSD sufferers.

All of these works are © copyrighted and protected please by the author, David Rose. For permission to use these poems in an educational venue, please contact the author at davidrose@gmail.com. Every reasonable request will be granted.

It is my sincere wish that you appreciate these poems to gain a better understanding of the thoughts, feelings and emotions of PTSD diseased patients. Here is my story…

I was drafted into the Army in 1969 during the time of the Vietnam War. Having a conservative Christian upbringing and a love for God, I chose to sign in as a conscientious objector and not carry a weapon.

In Vietnam I was stationed in the central highlands in Pleiku. I worked in the Emergency Room of the 71st Evacuation Hospital, a large 450 bed first line of emergency care. I also flew temporary duty (TDY) as a medic for the 283rd Dust Off (Medivac Helicopter) unit attached to our hospital.

In addition to my normal duties, I volunteered to donate my one-day off per week to hike into the jungle to four Montagnard villages to provide a sick call with some basic first aid and medical care.

In 1970 the 71st Evac was being phased out so I was transferred to Chu Lai on the coast to the 91st Evac. Hospital where I continued to work in the Emergency Room as a medic.

To give you just a baseline understanding of my PTSD source, I have three PTSD issues. 1. My war experiences themselves, 2. A survivor's guilt and 3. The disrespectful manner in which I was treated when I returned back home.

Being a sheltered conservative late teenager, a war situation was a lot for a young kid to face. I had to grow up fast.

When I returned home, I brought the war back with me. I couldn't cope with the real world anymore. I chose to not use drugs or alcohol. I chose to use busyness as my medication. I ran from the feelings and emotions that I didn't know how to manage. 45 years later all of this is catching up with me and I have seeked treatment from the VA for my PTSD disease.

Respectfully,

David L. Rose

David Rose, Author

Table of Contents

Experiencing War as a Man of Peace

As a young man, heard Desmond Doss speak
Wounded three times, but had a winning streak
Won the Medal of Honor, for his gallant performance
Conscientious Objector, and not a conformance

Learned a lot from him about courage and strength
Read his book and listened at length
Couldn't think of a better earthly example
Desmond's life lessons are really quite ample

Later in life, I did poorly in school
Goofed off a lot, acted a fool
Made poor grades, but had the knowledge
Drew a low number, was drafted from college

As a conservative Christian, had many objections
The military, weapons and the war, are my
recollections
Don't worry, take the white-coats someone said
But the dread of war, is what filled my head

Signed in, as a Conscientious Objector
Thought that was better, than being a defector
Considered Canada, didn't want a shaded past
Wanted to serve my country, when I was asked

Gained lots of respect, from day one
Just because I wouldn't carry a gun
No one asked for any explaining
Was chosen as leader at basic training

Long plane ride across the sea
What aid could this kid be
With such a violent land to trod
Armed only with the Word of God

Being unarmed was ok with me
Can't think of a time when I needed to be
Had my Bible in my shirt
And my War Angel on red alert

With a team like that, how can one lose
"Though shalt not kill" is what I choose
That's the Word by which I live
Answered prayers He will give

Most people didn't know I was a CO
Stayed too busy to be a GI Joe
Too busy saving lives
My mission was who survives

Don't know who's right and who's not
God still loves even those who fought
Ironic they died off one by one
When the only survivor didn't carry a gun

David Rose - Vietnam Veteran - Combat Medic

Forty-Five Years of Tears and Fears

Seems I have that PTSD bit
As was diagnosed by the VA
Thought I'd write a poem about it
Will try to focus today

This may have a negative tone
Just want to say before I start
I now have a stone
Where I once had a heart

Did my job well in that damn war
Thought I was a hero
Don't know what I fought for
Turned out I was a zero

Didn't know how to cope
So I decided to run
Chose not to use dope
If I'd chosen food I'd weigh a ton

Rarely get any good rest
Cause pain meds keep me flying
Even though I know it's not best
Cause there's things worse than dying

Afraid of having nightmares
Have them most every night
Am I the only one who cares
Sometimes I even fight

Don't meet with friends anymore
Can't follow their conversation
Hardly walk out the door
Just don't have the motivation

"Join a gym" my doctor said
"You won't feel so down"
Seldom crawl out of bed
Much less drive into town

Docs ask if I think about suicide
What sort of question is that
My moods change like the tide
And at the drop of a hat

Don't know where all this is taking me
Hope it's not here to stay
A year from now where will I be
Please God. Just get me through today

David Rose - Vietnam Veteran - Combat Medic

That's My War Angel Working

Long plane ride across the sea
Armed only with the Word of God
What aid could this kid be
With such a land to trod

Put my training to the test
To be the best I can
Want to be the very best
Not like Lt. Dan

Jumped into the deep end
No slow break-in for me
We had a hill to defend
Don't know where the gooks will be

One of my brothers took a round
Hit him in the chest
He's bleeding on the ground
Ran to him before the rest

Keeping my head low
Running from man to man
Seems I'm moving slow
But doing all I can

Got to know one kid well
Was hit and died in my arm
This place is really hell
Several bought the farm

Got beat up pretty bad
More of them than us
Used all the supplies I had
Called in the air bus

One asked me to make a call
Report his death to his son
A task that took my all
Toughest thing I've done

Too much for a 20 year old kid
Lots of dangers lurking
Surprised to survive as I did
That's my war angel working

David Rose - Vietnam Veteran - Combat Medic

My lighter for smoking dope during the war.

On PTSD Therapy

It's not about what I have done
Then living my life on the run
It's about what I have begun
Hope someday will overcome

David Rose - Vietnam Veteran - Combat Medic

PTSD

Panicked
Troubled
Solitary
Depressed

David Rose - Vietnam Veteran - Combat Medic

War Will Win

Lots of ways to die in war
Some worse than others
Lots die for what they stand for
Some die for their war brothers

Lots die in the act of war
Some will make it home
Lots live life in a candy store
Some find a need to roam

Lots find death rapid in war
Some deaths take a long time
Lots find life after war a chore
Some have a big hill to climb

Lots die some
Some die lots
No matter how or when you succumb
War will win at taking your life somehow

David Rose - Vietnam Veteran - Combat Medic

Thank You Friendly Sergeant

While on duty at the 71st
We rotate through Charge of Quarters
From the beginning, my duty was cursed
For we soon had incoming mortars

Soon to follow was intense ground fire
A friendly on the ground radioed me
Warned: "expect enemy through your wire"
He could tell I was a CO medic draftee

Didn't have to call a soul
Everyone sprang into action
I really had little control
There was little interaction

I manned the communications
Coordinated with friendlies outside
The armed manned their stations
Providing fire from the inside

Another round of mortars coming in
Together with a rush was their plan
It was clear a fight was soon to begin
Someone yelled, "Get that lead man."

Friendly sergeant radioed to say
They were coming in from behind
That would save the day
If our forces could be combined

Enemy was soon surrounded
Sergeant radioed for us to take cover
Until the all clear sounded
And the gun battle was over

It didn't take the friendlies long
Lots of enemy wounded and dead
Only a few remained of the Vietcong
Some of them fled

Lead man was our hospital barber
Had a pass to our compound
Seems he wanted another Pearl Harbor
Grenades strapped to his chest, wasn't messing 'round

We think they were after our Medivac
Had a map to go right to them
But they are all still in tact
Couldn't get to them this AM

Mortars caused one fire
Our only loss was that flame
It's that friendly sergeant I admire
Never met him, never knew his name

Seemed to show up from nowhere
He sure did help our crew
We didn't have any men to spare
All I can say is "Thank You"

David Rose - Vietnam Veteran - Combat Medic

I'd Do It All Again

Survived the Vietnam War
But lost my life

Traveled to come home
But never left

Loved coming home
But hated my reception

Thought I was a hero
Turned out I was really a zero

Hated that damn war
But loved my brothers

Multiple marriages
But none knew me

One wife asked if I was a spy
Or with the CIA

Lots of acquaintances
But no friends

Lots hired me
But lots fired me

Done lots of things
But for the wrong reasons

Been lots of places
But haven't seen much

Made lots of people laugh
But wanted to make them cry

Survived forty-five years
But died forty-five times

God kept me alive for a reason
But I'd do it all again if my country wanted me

David Rose - Vietnam Veteran - Combat Medic

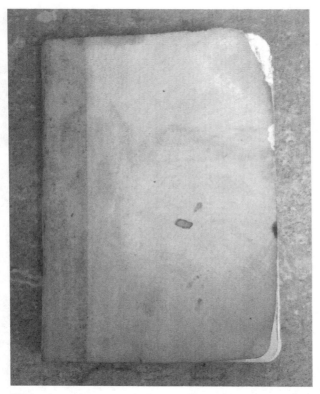

This is what remains of my pocket Bible that I had with me at all times. It is really beat up and covered in blood, but it was a comfort to my comrades and myself.

Poem From a PTSD Vet

David Rose - Vietnam Veteran - Combat Medic

Conversations with PTSD

With my PTSD I live in two consciousness's. One you can see on the surface and the second running full time in the background that may not be as obvious.

Here is an illustration of how a routine casual conversation goes for me. My words and thoughts are in all caps.

Friend, "Hello Dave. How are you?
Me, "I AM WELL THANKS."
Friend, "Hey I had a great vacation last week."
Yeah, I took my family down to Gulf Port.
We met some other family there from...SAY?
The weather there during our stay was...JUST SAY?
I did a little deep sea fishing there...HE JUST SAY??
I caught a Grouper, Red Snapper,...DID HE JUST SAY?
We were out djwk hbc j r...WHAT DID HE JUST SAY?
Yur fdrwt vfhty zswqy...NOW CONCENTRATE AND LISTEN TO WHAT HE IS SAYING?
Grftu jnkfl vgrws mnkp...WHAT IF HE ASKS ME A QUESTION?
Hgds vgdtru bgdwqa nkplyr jkyt...OH NO. I AM COMPLETELY GONE NOW.
Gbtry cfgdryt hbjkumn fgdrtey lkjmnhg...HOW CAN I GET OUT OF THIS GRACEFULLY?

David Rose - Vietnam Veteran - Combat Medic

I'd write a title
But I just can't think of one right now

I'd write a song about PTSD
But I'd never remember the words

I'd exercise more
But I rarely feel like getting out of bed

I'd eat more
But sometimes it's just too much trouble

I'd go to the movies
But they trigger too many emotions

I'd have more friends
But I end up pushing them away somehow

I'd sleep at night
But I'm afraid of my nightmares

I'd go out to dinner
But I guess I'll just get a bag of chips and go to my
room

I'd answer the phone
But I usually just let it go to voicemail

I'd grocery shop at BI-LO
But I shop at 0300 so I go to Wal-Mart

I'd visit my bank
But I do all of my banking at an ATM after midnight

I'd talk on the phone
But I'd rather text

I'd drive my car
But I'm too distracted and dangerous

I'd take my meds
But they accentuate my feelings instead of correcting
them

I'd do my work
But I can't concentrate or motivate

I'd sleep with my wife
But I sometimes hit her in the night

I'd write another line here
But I just can't concentrate long enough

David Rose - Vietnam Veteran - Combat Medic

Try It. You Vill Like It

So I have this PTSD disease
Oh you need to go see Dr. Burress
Asked may I have some meds please
Said it's my feelings I want to suppress

Let's start you out slow
Don't want to hit you with the big stuff yet
I'll make adjustments as we go
Depending on the type of side effects you get

Gave me something called a Zoloft pill
He said "Try it. You vill like it"
Better update my living will
Is this doctor legit

All of my meds come in this little white sack
Postmaster said, "David your maracas came in today"
Said, "Yeah I'm joining a Mexican band called Smack"
Come hear us we open soon in Monterey

Took the first pill in the morning
By five o'clock I didn't care about a single thing
That should have been a clear warning
Just forget having a fling

Went back to see my doc
Said I don't like these side effects
This med is a real crock
He said, "I have somezing we try next"

He said, "Try it. You vill like it"
Take them in the morning and at night
Those others you can quit

This time it will be all right
Took them for a few days
Didn't feel a single thing
Thought maybe there were delays
My ears didn't even ring

Went to see my doc again
Said I want a big boy hit
He said "I have somezing for you to begin"
He said, "Try it. You vill like it"

He said I overnight to you
As you are very depressed
You vill feel better when you come too
You vill soon feel your best

Start out slow, cut one pill in two
Took my meds as the doc said
Don't want it to be too much for you
Take it just before bed

Yeah right, bring it on doc
What could this little pill do
When I laid down, I looked at the clock
It was about twenty-four hours later when I came too

Damn! What hit me I said
I'm dizzy as I can be
And what's wrong with my head
I can't possibly be me

No way can I walk
I can hardly move,
And I can barely talk
Sure hope I improve

Just give me my PTSD back
I'm learning to deal with it
I'd rather have the panic attack
Than take this pill and have a fit

I meet with my doc again in a bit
I'll say, "Here you go Jack.
Try it. You vill like it"
Then I will give his damn pills back

David Rose - Vietnam War - Combat Medic

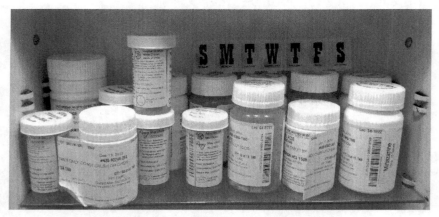

My VA PTSD medicine cabinet. Wow.

Got To Go

Called to Cambodia, a place called "Fish Hook"
Lots of boys down, thought about taking the Chinook
Very hot area, called gun ships for cover
Need their big guns, while they hover

On radio with the ground, to establish a plan
"Brought escorts, will set down when we can"
All medics are dead, no support there
Will need help, from any men you can spare

Unbelievable, what damage done
Sucking chest wound, head wound on one
Mortar in mans chest, a double amputee
One-man unconscious, another can't see

Gun ships go in first, to clear the way
Three gun ships can create quite a display
I had not experienced an escort before
I don't want to fly without them, anymore

Lots of noise all around, then somebody yelled "GO!"
We came in hot and low, now my time to show
No time to spare, pilot said I had one minute
Had to move all four men within it

Hit the ground, in a run
Moved the men one by one
Pilot started yelling "GOT TO GO, GOT TO GO!"
Loaded in less than a minute I know

While on the ground I was full speed ahead
Could feel enemy fire flying past my head
It must have been a tumbling round
The shock wave was quite profound

These men were dying, had to move fast
Little room to move, but got around at last
Starting IV's and stopping the bleeding
So far I was succeeding

We were cruising fast at treetop
Didn't want Charley to hear our chop
Gun ships all around us
That sure was a plus

I heard ground fire penetrate the under side
Wasn't sure yet what that implied
Pilot said, "I'm hit and the controls are sloppy"
"Might have to ditch this ole jalopy"

Cleared the trees just in time
Pilot said, "We can't climb!"
"Brace for impact" is what he said
"Might be crashing on our head!"

Skidded into a rice field
Lucky but now unconcealed
Shut the engine down
Prepared to move by ground

Gun ships hovered around to give us a hand
Distribute the wounded is what we planned
Had to move fast, before we were zeroed in
Crew chiefs came to help us, the move to begin

Got all the wounded reloaded
Must exit area, before it's exploded
Flying away I peeked out the door
Looked back, our helicopter was no more

Flew our wounded back to the 71st
With the ER I conversed
All in all, it was quite an ordeal
A better choice of words might be "surreal"

It were the gun ships that made the day
Needed them to make our way
No medics on the ground
But the troops rallied 'round

One task remains before our mission is complete
I have the pilot yet to treat
Removed the frag from his calf
We were flying back again, in an hour and a half

David Rose - Vietnam Veteran - Combat Medic

PS.
I recall all this in extreme detail
I can still feel every inhale
Reliving in slow motion
I remember all the commotion

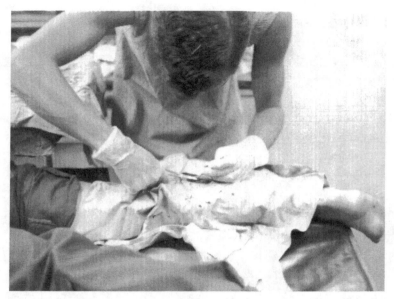

Doing surgery on my pilot's leg removing frag.

The frag.

I Had A Dream Last Night

I had a dream last night
Different from my usual plight

Instead of nightmares about the war
There was something I had to look for

Since many of our men were MIA
I had an act of respect to convey

I set out to find a marker stone
Perhaps the largest one even known

Traveled all over this old earth
To seek a stone of proper girth

Moved it to the beach near Chu Lai
To mark the country where our brothers die

It was one hundred meters high
And escaped no ones eye

On it I carved "Here Lies Our Best"
"Have Peace While You Rest"

"We Will Never Forget"
"You Are In Our Debt"

The stone will always be in the light
The sun by day and the stars by night

No rain cloud will ever get it wet
Yet flowers grow around it you can bet

Storms will come and storms will go
But on this stone no winds will blow

This is a very special stone
Our brothers are no longer left alone

Different from my usual plight
I had a dream last night

David Rose - Vietnam Veteran - Combat Medic

Heli-pad outside our Emergency Room front door.

The Nature of PTSD

Like fording a flowing river,
Can knock you off your feet.
I went from a busy socialite,
To a man in full retreat.

Like a cloudy dark night,
Can make you loose direction.
I feel I have traveled beyond,
A late-in-life intersection.

Like a raptor on the hunt,
Flying high to survey the ground.
I stay hyper vigilant,
And watch people all around.

Like the bears during winter,
Finding shelter in a cave.
I have to protect myself,
From those emotions that rave.

Like the innocents of a sparrow
Living a simple life
I seek to find some peace again
Instead of all this strife

Like the midnight darkness,
Waiting for the sun to rise.
I long to live my life again,
With clear unclouded skies.

Like wind blowing the clouds away,
And the grey skies turning blue.
I want my normal life back,
To start it all anew.   David Rose

Recognition Or Acceptance

My therapist thinks it's recognition I seek
Minimizing my PTSD so to speak
"Won't get any praise from the VA"
Is what my therapist had to say

Exiting the plane from Vietnam
I just wanted to get home to see mom
Didn't really know what to expect
Never dreamt I'd receive such disrespect
Was I seeking recognition then?

Hospitalized for shell shock in 71 & 73
Before PTSD was yet to be
Stress so great I was bleeding inside
All VA support back then was fully denied
Was I seeking recognition then?

Didn't know what to do with myself
Put my emotions away on the shelf
Decided to run for the next 45 years
But now here come the tears
Was I seeking recognition then?

Tears have hit me seemingly overnight
Impressive what a change PTSD can incite
This is nothing I asked for
Just long-term side affects of a lousy war
Was I seeking recognition then?

When I stay in bed all day from depression
Or when I speak with a lot of aggression
When I can't do my work all day
Because my concentration goes away

Am I seeking recognition then?
When I startle in fear
Thinking danger is near
When I sit in a defensive position
To anticipate the opposition
Am I seeking recognition then?

When I don't go to movies or watch TV
Because of what I might hear or see
When I shop in the middle of the night
Because I'm so uptight
Am I seeking recognition then?

When I have nightmares that awaken me
And get me up at three
When I have intrusive thoughts during the day
The horrible images they portray
Am I seeking recognition then?

When I volunteer at the Medal of Honor Museum
I'm not working in a coliseum
I'm as secluded as I can be
No one ever sees me
Am I seeking recognition then?

Through the decades I have even established
recognition
Support for our troops was my personal mission
I would be at the airport when our troops flew in
Even when none were next of kin
Am I seeking recognition then?

Perhaps my therapist is confusing acceptance with recognition
I've already stated that seeking camaraderie was an ambition
Trying to replace the honor we had during the war
I don't think it's out there. I don't look anymore

I'm not trying to contrive
I just want to survive
It's hard enough dealing with all of this
Without being thrown into the abyss

Don't send me off to war
Then treat me like a whore
Don't minimize how I feel today
By letting this recognition thing get in our way

David Rose - Vietnam Veteran - Combat Medic

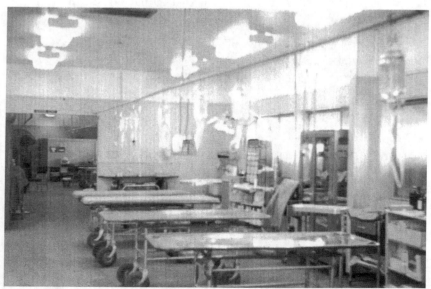

71st Evacuation Hospital ER in a rare idle state.

The Clock in the Hall

Ever sense this PTSD thing hit
I've been down in the pit
I stay pretty much secluded
From normal activities I'm excluded
Can't keep living life this way
Hope it's not here to stay

The clock keeps ticking on the wall
I can hear it down the hall

I see my friends moving along
Their lives are going strong
Life is going on elsewhere
Even though I'm not there
The more depressed I get
So in this room I sit

The clock keeps ticking on the wall
I can hear it down the hall

Life is passing me by
No matter how hard I try
It's hard to get going
With the symptoms I'm showing
Can't keep living life this way
Hope it's not here to stay

The clock keeps ticking on the wall
I can hear it down the hall

David Rose - Vietnam Veteran - Combat Medic

My Busyness Medicine

Have to run now
To distance my emotions somehow
Not sure of what to do with everything I was feeling
My intrusive thoughts kept me reeling

Ran to and fro doing this and that
Trying to forget about all that combat
Built a big house and drove a fast race car
Formed a company and traveled afar

Wrote books about a cliché'
Took surgery call almost every day
Produced many musical concerts
Built a satellite network to gain new converts

Worked every wake hour with my dot com
Trying to forget about that Vietnam
Extreme busyness was my deal
Didn't know the right way to heal

David Rose - Vietnam Veteran - Combat Medic

Removing All External Stress

I've seen all kinds of doctors for this PTSD thing
In anticipation of the healing they could bring
I have a doctor to prescribe my med
I have doctors who get into my head

I have a doctor for one on ones
I have a doctor for a group he runs
I may have more doctors but I forget
I even have a doctor I haven't met yet

I sincerely appreciate all they do for me
Each one is as helpful as they can be
Maybe my meds will start to plateau
Maybe the counseling will do it, I don't know

As I study all of this to hopefully find a cure
There is one thing I have learned for sure
Before I can get out of this big mess
I need to remove all external stress

I don't really have a choice in the matter
This is nothing about which to smatter
40% of PTSD Vets take their own lives
Just a very small number survives

I was killed fourth-five years ago
I'm just dying real slow
I've never seriously considered taking my own life
But I can understand how other people do with all this
strife

I still have a strong sense to survive
My family needs me alive
To establish a somewhat positive outlook
I need to reduce stress by hook or crook

I've considered a life like the "Jeremiah Johnson"
movie
Living in the mountains sounds pretty groovy
Even that movie "Castaway" sounds healing
Yes maybe extreme, but nonetheless appealing

The bottom line is simply this
I may never again experience true bliss
But I think I could manage my PTSD with better
success
If I could just eliminate all of this external stress

David Rose - Vietnam Veteran - Combat Medic

My baggage claim ticket from my trip back home.

I Know of a Hero

Not I, but I know of a hero who...
Threw himself on a grenade in the mud
Fortunately for him, it was a dud.

Not I, but it know of a hero who...
Flew his helicopter in with enemy all around
Tried to fly away, was shot to the ground.

Not I, but I know of a hero who...
Threw his body on a grenade to soften the blast
Gave of his own life so others will last.

Not I, but I know of a hero who...
Shot six snipers, plus two more by hand
Sacrificed himself, while his platoon made a stand.

Not I, but I know of a hero who...
Made five charges to create a perimeter gap
Enabling his company to exit the trap

Not I, but I know of a hero who...
Encouraged and directed his men where to return fire
Pushed back the enemy outside the wire

Not I, but I know of a hero who...
Positioned himself to protect his friend
Watched the enemy aim, knowing it's the end

Not I, but I know of a hero who...
Sees a grenade come in, his own life to give
Covers with his helmet, all men will live

Not I, but I know of a hero who...
Single handily reduced the enemy into defeat
Provided cover, while the wounded made a retreat

Not I, but I know of a hero who...
Fell on a grenade and survived the blast
Gave aid to his comrade, as he passed

Not I, but I know of a hero who...
Pulled the wounded to safety, giving CPR as he went
Aided his comrades, until he himself was spent

Not I, but I know of a hero who...
Pilot can't survive the crash, but the navigator can
Ditched plane in the water, to save the other man

Not I, but I know of a hero who...
Destroyed 10 enemy bunkers and more
Saved his own life, and those of his corps

Not I, but I know of a hero who...
Utilized 3 helicopters, to evacuate 51
It's hard to comprehend what he had just done

Not I, but I know of a hero who...
Caught an incoming grenade and held it to his chest
Saved 3 of his comrades, from the blast he
suppressed

Not I, but I know of a hero who...
Was seriously wounded and driven to win
Took a rocket, to do him in

Not I, but I know of a hero who...
Destroyed a bunker and performed without a flaw

Forcing enemy troops, to quickly withdraw
Not I, but I know of a hero who...
Organized a retreat to save his men
Went back in, to do it all again

Not I, but I know of a hero who...
Malfunctioned his grenade, seconds to react
To save his platoon, he absorbed the impact

Not I, but I know of a hero who...
Was a POW who adhered to the code
Gained respect from the enemy, for the valor he
showed

Not I, but I know of a hero who...
Rolled over on grenade so comrades wouldn't pass
away
Energized his team, to defeat the NVA

Not I, but I know of a hero who...
Crossed a river to recover his wounded when success
was slim
Moved them all to safety, even though he couldn't
swim

Not I, but I know of a hero who...
Kept his damaged jet in the air to complete his mission
Silenced the enemy defensive position

David Rose - Vietnam Veteran - Combat Medic

His Big Scar

As an ER medic in Nam
We kind of did our own thing
Nobody really gave a damn
They let us have our fling

I wore custom tailored pants
And let my hair grow long
Funny what privilege grants
Been wearing a scrub shirt all along

One day I decided to walk into town
Don't remember what I went for
Maybe just to walk around
Didn't know I had a surprise in store

A new MP stopped me in his Jeep
And threw me over the hood
I didn't make a peep
Why he handcuffed me I never understood

Hauled me to the MP station
And pushed me through the front door
Told the sergeant there I was getting a citation
Because he didn't like the uniform I wore

Sergeant said, "That's Doc Rose.
Why are you bringing him in?
Don't worry about his cloths."
That poor MP couldn't win

Sergeant said, "Take Doc wherever he wants to go
And take off that damn handcuff!"
There is no way that poor MP could know

That he didn't have to get tough
About a week later, that same MP came into the ER
Seems he cut his hand and finger
Was going to be treated by Dr. Spencer
I told him, "Doc I got this one. No need to linger."

I comforted the MP as routine
Told him he would feel no pain
As I drew up some saline
Instead of Novocain

I said "Let me know if any of this hurts.
I can give you more pain killer."
It's amazing the control he exerts
He was as rigid as a pillar

He toughed it out
While the nursing staff was giggling
Not once did he shout
He wasn't even wiggling

Every once in a while
Someone whipped the sweat off his brow
He even mustered a smile
He got through it somehow

To become friends is what we requested
Saw him often in the ER
I'd joke about getting arrested
He'd joke about his big scar

David Rose - Vietnam Veteran - Combat Medic

Gaining Insight

Now that I have studied this PTSD for a while
I can reflect and understand why I've been so hostile
There were numerous times throughout my life
When I have created unnecessary strife

Sometimes when I would open my mouth
The conversation would turn south
If I had to make an important decision
It may be based on a wartime vision

Many of my civilian engagements were wrong
Because my head was where it didn't belong
I lost a lot in life because of all of this
It's painful to look back and realize what all I missed

Strained relationships with family and friends
I hope it's not too late to make amends
I was protecting myself from them and them from me
Back then it was the only way I knew how to be

I'm not saying I have all of the answers yet
But I'll take all the little nuggets I can get
I still have a long way to go
But at least I'm gaining insight about things I need to
know

David Rose - Vietnam Veteran - Combat Medic

My PTSD Septic Tank is Busted

When I built my PTSD house 45 years ago
I installed a septic tank down below

A lot of poop has built up over the decades
Not all of it degrades

One day I thought I smelled something fishy
Went outside and the lawn was all squishy

Repairman said the tank had a crack
Would cost me a lot of jack

Decided to not repair it now
Would mask the smell somehow

City inspector said, "Codes are not being met"
I said, "Recent rains made the lawn that wet"

Soon the neighbors started to complain
Said I was contaminating the terrain

Later the toilet started to flow over
Because of all that poop out in the clover

Decided to use the toilet upstairs
To avoid those costly repairs

One day I came home and opened the front door
Got covered in poop from that damn war

David Rose - Vietnam Veteran - Combat Medic
Inspired by Dr. Lefton (VA Mental Health)

A Man of the Moon

Considering becoming a man of the moon
The opposite of living life around noon
What difference would it make
The time of day I am awake

The night provides better cover
More like living life undercover
I seem to have fewer triggers then
That I experience during day time and again

I run my errands at night now anyway
The things I used to do during the day
Like grocery shopping and going to the bank
It's even midnight when I put gas in the tank

There are far fewer people about
And much less traffic in route
During the day I hear car horns and phones ringing
At night I hear the leaves rustling and birds singing

The night is a more peaceful time in which to live
I'm also attracted to the solitude it can give
The night just offers more of what I need right now
I'm seriously considering making it work somehow

David Rose - Vietnam Veteran - Combat Medic

Hit Me Broadside

I was just walking along one day
Spending time in my usual way
When along came this Greyhound bus
It must have been doing seventy plus

I didn't see it coming
Didn't know I'd be succumbing
No way to avoid the collide
The thing hit me broadside

Sent me flying and landed on my head
At least I'm not dead
Felt like I was hit between the eyes
With all of the complications that implies

Even though this is an analogy tale
It illustrates how PTSD can strongly prevail
Long recovery from a bus wreck
Long recovery from PTSD I expect

David Rose - Vietnam Veteran - Combat Medic

Rice Wine To Go

Worked six days a week in the ER
On my day off I'd hike out to where the Montagnards
are
I volunteered to conduct a sick call
As they didn't have modern medical support at all

I didn't carry a weapon as a CO
So I had an infantryman assigned to me when I go
I would hike through the jungle on the trail
Not knowing what each journey would entail

My first stop at each village had to be the Elder's Hut
I had to comply with their native customs somewhat
So i joined them in their rice wine drinking tradition
Until I was of a drunken condition

They even provided meals for me to eat
Wild boar and corn on the cob that couldn't be beat
Everything they served me to eat was just fine
Then they brought me a cup of guess what, more rice
wine

After all of that I did manage a sick call, I think
If I needed a consult I always had a radio link
I remember finding a few diagnoses that made the
effort worthwhile
Even carried a few back to the hospital once in a while

I made friends with the elders over the course of the
year
The drinking was new to me, I had never even tasted
beer
We couldn't communicate verbally but we really didn't
care
Our game of charades was pretty fair

My last visit there was a memory to forever cherish
Because of a friendship that would never perish
They gave me a Montagnards blanket and all the
children danced in a row
They gave me something else to, can you guess what,
some rice wine to go

David Rose - Vietnam Veteran - Combat Medic

Me eating that wonderful corn on the cob.

Me drinking rice wine from a big pot.

Me performing sick call.

My bodyguard giving himself a sick call after too much rice wine. Some bodyguard huh?

My Montagnard blanket gift on display in the National Medal of Honor of Military History Museum.

Please Don't Tell Anyone

I have a ninety-year-old father who lives with me
He has pain in his back and in his knee

His doctor gave him this Percocet pill
He said, "ask anytime for a refill"

I was struggling one day
Needed to keep my daemons away

Decided to try one and take a chance
Seemed like a reasonable idea at first glance

Made me feel warm everywhere
Had more conversation to share

It really gave me the boost I needed
My idea had succeeded

Percocet allows me to feel happy
Instead of being so snappy

I understand all the reasons it's wrong
Some days I just need a little help to get along

I haven't started anything that can't be undone
PS. Please don't tell anyone

David Rose - Vietnam Veteran - Combat Medic

Celebrating Memorial Day with PTSD

I've appreciated dozens of Memorial Days
I've celebrated it in lots of ways

I've been to the Indy 500
I've been treasure hunting and wrongly plundered

I've toured the Greek countryside
I've crossed the great divide

I've stayed home and had a Bar-B-Q
I've even worked all the way thru

I've respected Memorial Day all these years
I've experienced cheers and tears

I've remembered my fallen brothers from the war
I've shared my esprit de corps

I've today experienced Memorial Day with PTSD
I've definitely become much more of a devotee

David Rose - Vietnam Veteran - Combat Medic

Through The Holy Spirit

I keep hearing that this PTSD is here to stay
My only hope is to try to cope in some way

These memories are embedded in my brain
Sometimes they make me feel insane

Medication hasn't helped me yet
They could be more of a threat

I've had private one on one sessions
From multiple professions

I've had therapy in a Vietnam War group
That just brings up a lot of old poop

I wish my mother was still alive
She could tell me how to thrive

She was a counselor too
But from a Christian point of view

She kept a journal just before she died
It wasn't much but she really tried

She had written only a few pages
That little bit truly engages

She said, "Develop a mindset of constant prayer.
With the Holy Spirit be aware."

Even though she didn't write much
My heart she did touch

Luke 4:18 says, "With the Spirit be infused
To set at liberty them that are bruised"

Through the Holy Spirit we can heal
And survive any challenging ordeal

David Rose - Vietnam Veteran - Combat Medic

The Three P's of PTSD Life

Depression is living life in the **P**ast
Peace is living life in the **P**resent
Anxiety is living life in the **P**rospective

David Rose - Vietnam Veteran - Combat Medic
Inspired by Dr. Jackson

One Doctor's Diagnosis

I'm not stressed because I have PTSD,
I have PTSD because I'm stressed.

David Rose
Inspired by Dr. Burress

Just a Jerk

Diagnosed with PTSD about seven months ago
Because of my experiences as a GI Joe

I think I have seen nine doctors if I remember right
The VA has lots of doctors on site

My PCP discovered my plight first
She sent me to another doctor who was better versed

He said, "My job is to reconfirm"
"I am just short term"

He said, "Meds are what you need"
"We have another doctor for that who will intercede"

These meds have no guarantees
They could be worse than the disease

Long-term therapy is what you should get
You have another doctor for that too I'll bet

After many months of one on one
It's now time to bring in the big gun

You need to start group therapy now
I think it will help you somehow

This doctor is a Vietnam Vet too
He may have a better clue for you

There is even talk of sending me to Kentucky
An intensive program with good results if I'm lucky

OK. Now go see a doctor for an Agent Orange exam
Had one two months ago, but forgot where I am

That first doctor's exam was for the AO Registry
This doctor is whom you really need to see

Nice to have all this high-powered examination
But then have some high school dropout do my claim
evaluation

What happens if after all of this work,
These doctors decide I'm not sick at all, I'm just a jerk?

David Rose - Vietnam Veteran - Combat Medic

Sign over the front door of the Emergency Room
where I was stationed in Pleiku, Vietnam.

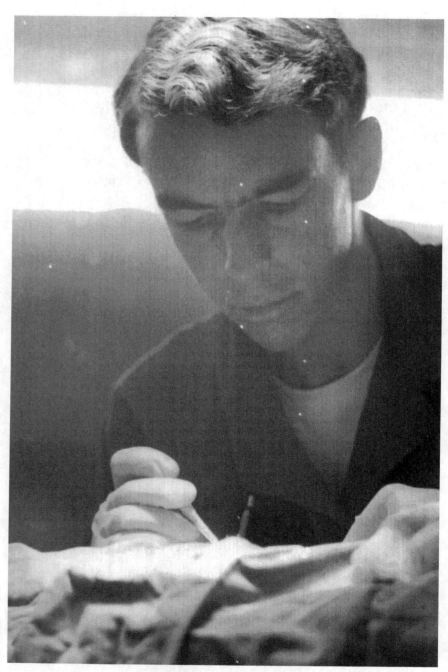

David Rose, the author, performing minor surgery at the 71st Evacuation Hospital in Pleiku, Vietnam in 1970.

Through Tender Mercy

I have been reading this text all my life
Didn't apply it to the life I had known
Now that I have developed all this strife
I can now apply it to a need of my own

Luke 1:78-79
78 Through the tender mercy of our God,
whereby the dayspring from on high hath visited us,
79 To give light to them that sit in darkness and in the
shadow of death, to guide our feet into the way of
peace.

David Rose

Prayer of a Vietnam Veteran

Dear Jesus and my Heavenly Father above
Creator of all things and source of all love

There are lots of things I want and need to say
But for right now please just get me through today

Amen

David Rose - Vietnam Veteran - Combat Medic

Just Leave A Message

There is something I don't understand yet
Something about this PTSD I just can't get
That is why I can't follow a conversation
At least not for any reasonable duration

If somebody talks too fast there is no hope
I just stand there looking like a dope
I couldn't repeat what they said if I had to
I tried to listen but really don't have a clue

I think it has to do with my concentration
Not my friends' quality of oration
There is a limit to how long I can stay in tune
When I reach my cap I'm finished too soon

I don't want to look like a fool
Don't want my friends to think I'm uncool
So I protect myself from them and them from me
Total seclusion is my self-surviving plea

It's not that I don't want to talk to you, I do
It's just frustrating for me to not connect with you
So if you want to talk, I'll give you a little presage
Call me and you will have to just leave a message

David Rose - Vietnam Veteran - Combat Medic

The Poetic Police

I enjoy writing these lines
And it's good therapy too.
I enjoy poetry of all kinds.
It gives me something to do.

Something I have learned since I started,
Is that the poetic police will find you.
They are all being good hearted.
They all want to do a review.

One said, "I'll take a quick look
And let you know what I think."
I'm like, "OK you can read my book.
Just remember. You're not my shrink."

He said, "I think they are awfully good"
Isn't that one of those oxymoron things?
I don't want to be misunderstood.
I like all the support this brings.

He said, " Your poems have casual authenticity."
What does that mean?
I know I write with simplicity.
I want to keep my writings routine.

Another person said, "I will proof read for you"
"I will send you the corrected version."
I really appreciate all that they do.
They've been helpful since I started this poetic
excursion.

I'm really not trying to win any awards now.
I just jot down my thoughts as they arise,
To try to help my veteran brothers somehow.
I'm not trying to win the Nobel Peace Prize.

I really don't care if I am missing a little dot here or
there,
Or that little curvy one they call a comma.
At least the poetic police really do care.
Next, I will probably hear from Barack Obama.

David Rose - Vietnam Veteran - Combat Medic

Not Yet

I'm not yet where I want to be with this PTSD.
But thank God,
My PTSD is not where it used to be.

David Rose - Vietnam Veteran - Combat Medic
Inspired by Dr. Sandy McKenzie

Anger and PTSD

PTSD doesn't make my anger
Anger makes my PTSD

David Rose - Vietnam Veteran - Combat Medic
Inspired by a Vietnam War brother

Me and my guitar in Chu Lai, Vietnam.

Inside To Stay

I took a personality test one time years ago
Personalities like mine are almost zero

Yeah, I'm introverted but so what
I won't run around like some nut

With me it's not about being odd
It's about creating a facade

I have junk in my head I don't want you to see
I'm protecting me from you and you from me

You may never learn who I am
After all that war in Vietnam

One wife asked if I was a spy
Of if I worked with the CIA on the sly

Don't take it personal if I just walk away
There are words I don't want you to hear me say

You can study my fingerprints in detail
And you won't learn what my thoughts entail

You can search my home everywhere
And you will come up bare

Read my CV all the way through
And you won't find a single clue

Follow me around day and night
You won't discover a single hint of my plight

Ask my friends. They'll say I'm cool
They'll say I'm no fool

There are two parts to me it seems
I don't want to carry the troubled one to extremes

It's a lot better this way
My thoughts are inside to stay

David Rose - Vietnam Veteran - Combat Medic

D-Toured

Was cruising along life's smooth road
Until my coping vehicle slowed
Encountered a PTSD-Tour
This side trip wasn't in the brochure

This detour is rocky, dusty and curvy
Has me going all topsy-turvy
Hope this detour road is not very long
The wide smooth blacktop is where I belong

David Rose - Vietnam Veteran - Combat Medic

Where Is PTSD Safe?

Where is PTSD safe?
Should my own home be a chafe?
My home needs a PTSD safe room,
One that's free of gloom and doom.

My father and former spouse live with me.
When I come home, CNN is blaring on the TV.
Wolfe is on some war rant about who knows what.
The sound of automatic weapons hits me in the gut.

I've already had two hours of VA group,
Then come home to all of this poop.
Most people are desensitized to war action.
I know I'm of a minute fraction.

My place is small but they each have their own room.
Having no safe place to go is what makes me fume.
So I sit in my one living room chair,
Put in my ear pods of music, close my eyes and stare.

I need a room with control over what I see and hear.
A place where all my bad thoughts will disappear.
I need a refuge where I can meditate and pray.
Where really is PTSD safe anyway?

David Rose - Vietnam Veteran - Combat Medic

Some Wounds Never Heal

Lots of ways to be wounded in war
Bullets, grenades, rockets and so much more

Some are mortally wounded and die right away
Take a big hit and don't last the day

Others are wounded but survive
Takes some time but they revive

There is one type of wound that you can't see
Just ask a few questions and you will agree

This wound stays with you for life
Infects, festers and causes real strife

Some survive it
Some commit

Regardless of the type wound you receive
War will kill you eventually I believe

David Rose - Vietnam Veteran - Combat Medic
Inspired by Dr. Jackson and the Vet Center slogan

Free: Living Heart Donor Available

I think I qualify as a living heart donor
My heart might like a new owner

My heart is still good for pumping blood
But instead of lub dub, it sounds more like thud thud

Here is what my massage therapist said
She said, "Your heart chakra is dead"

"Your capacity for love is gone."
"Your emotional bank account is overdrawn."

So if I'm not using all of my heart
Give it to someone who needs a spare part

It's a good heart with lots of love to give
It has lots of ticks on it with many more years to live

So if you want this old heart of mine
Just call 555.9999

David Rose - Vietnam Veteran - Combat Medic

It's Been Nice Knowing Y'all

Starting a new drug today for major depressive
disorder
The doctor said my thoughts are out of order
I'm not sure yet what to make of all this
I hope soon to be in true bliss

I looked up the side effects today
Not sure this drug is here to stay
This drug may be worse than the disease
I know it comes with no guarantees

I will have nausea and will be dizzy
I could sleep all day or run in a tizzy
I'll have dry mouth and constipation
Also headaches from the dehydration

Sounds bad huh, but that's not all
The sexual dysfunction sounds like a ball
This drug could even act in reverse
I could get a lot worse

Through all of these side effects I'm supposed to get
happy
And not be so snappy
I hope this works well for the long haul
If not, it's been nice knowing y'all

David Rose - Vietnam Veteran - Combat Medic

I'm Not Afraid Of Death

I just realized that I am not afraid of death.
What's so scary about taking your last breath?

I've already experienced the worst terror of my life,
Fear so thick I could cut it with a knife.

So how much more hell could one life provide,
Than a war in which I should have died?

I've experienced heaven and I've experienced hell.
Heaven is what I choose I know so well.

David Rose - Vietnam Veteran - Combat Medic

Started A New Happy Med Today

Started a new antidepressant from the VA.
Took it with a full supper today.

Doc said, "Take it with a full meal,
Because nausea is what you will feel."

Isn't that like eating a big breakfast before deep sea fishing?
As my head went over the rail, it was stable land I was wishing.

About four hours later the drug hit me.
Experienced some reactions I didn't foresee.

Felt like a big dark cloud moved in,
Blocking a spot in the sky where the sun had been.

My hands and face went numb.
To this new med I had just succumb.

"What's that you say?
I can't hear you till this ringing goes away."

Tried to stand up but sat right back down.
Threw up because my head was spinning round.

My pulse was 120 and my pressure was 154 over 103.
Tell me again how this med is so good for me?

Tried to go to bed to get some rest.
Couldn't do it for this thing pounding in my chest.

My hands are trembling so much,
These keys are tricky to touch.

So when is the payoff for me?
It's results I need to see.

Do I need to wade through this four more weeks,
Before my doctor critiques?

So remind me again why I am taking this.
Oh yeah. So I can experience true bliss.

David Rose - Vietnam Veteran - Combat Medic

It's Complicated

It's rather amazing how complicated PTSD is
There is a lot to consider in this tricky biz
I have memories of war fused in my brain
I still miss my buddies who were slain

My fight or flight response has been in play for
decades
Then there's that intrusive thought that pervades
I have survivors' guilt that hurts a lot
With all of the emotions that it brought

Became addicted to adrenaline in that damn war
In civilian life I chose to continue the gore
Did all kinds of things to feed that habit
Stayed busy running around like a rabbit

All kinds of chemicals circulating around
There is the man made compound
Can't forget the endogenous high
That can also make you fly

There's hyper vigilance and anxiety
There is avoidance of society
Also anger, boredom and grief
Disrespect for the Commander-in-Chief

Throw in the fact that I didn't know what was wrong
No wonder I didn't know where I belong
All of this sure did mess up my life
Now I know why I couldn't keep a wife

David Rose - Vietnam Veteran - Combat Medic

3 Glorious Minutes of Freedom

During the war we all got together to smoke dope.
It was every body's vehicle to cope.

We used an empty Quonset hut room.
Set up a big stereo with lots of boom.

Each night after supper we'd all gather 'round,
Pass the joints and crank up the sound.

Our theme song was "Our House" by CS&N.
We'd play it again and again and again.

Sometimes I'd stand up and conduct the song.
Everybody in the room would sing along.

One night recently I was driving a four-hour road trip.
"Our House" came of the radio and I thought I would
flip.

I sang at the top of my voice and pounded on the
dash.
Jumped in my seat and I'm surprised I didn't crash.

I laughed and cried at the same time.
For a few minutes there I felt sublime.

I became so emotional I pulled over by some big tree.
For a few glorious minutes... I was free, I was free, I
was free!

David Rose - Vietnam Veteran - Combat Medic

Sometimes I Close My Eyes

Sometimes I close my eyes and make my own
paradise
I crank up my stereo and dream of some place nice
I'll switch among my Pandora stations
I like the tunes I've been listening to for generations

It may be jazz, classic rock or classical guitar
No matter what it is I'm always the star
I'll sing along at the top of my voice
And playing air guitar is always my choice

I love to hear my 15-inch subwoofer rumble
This is not the time to be humble
Since I no longer visit saloons
One of my remaining joys is listening to my tunes

David Rose - Vietnam Veteran - Combat Medic

Cleanup On Aisle Three

Visited my local hardware store
Had to pickup something for a home chore

A song came over the PA that hit my trigger
I stood there and cried with vigor

Then I heard, "Cleanup on aisle three"
Didn't take them long to get a fix on me

David Rose - Vietnam Veteran - Combat Medic

Going Dark

I'm going dark today
Dropping out so to say
Protecting them from me
Is my new decree

I've had too much anger
I'm too much of a danger
Can't control my aggression
So I'm going into recession

It's not worth the stress
Is what I've assessed
So it's home to stay
Getting out of the way

I Don't Sit

I don't sit and think about my PTSD,
My PTSD thinks about me and I sit.

David Rose – Vietnam Veteran – Combat Medic

Why It's Called POST

During the war I could sleep anywhere
Today, a full nights rest is rare

Fifty years ago I slept leaned up on a tree
I slept through rain, mosquitoes and artillery

I slept through the hot scorching sun
I think I even slept while on the run

I have slept at noon
And I have slept through a typhoon

But today is a different story
I have nightmares that are gory

I have insomnia with a roof over my head
Tucked into my own warm bed

I have a woman next to me who is a dear
But I still can't sleep for all of this fear

This must be why it's called POST Disorder
My reality sure is out of order

Please Don't Ask Me Why

There are some words you shouldn't say
Like...are you OK?

Don't ask what's wrong
If you want us to get along

Don't ask why I sit here
When I drink my beer

If I don't watch the news
I could have a short fuse

If I react and lash out
Don't ask what I'm angry about

Any second I could start to cry
Please don't ask me why

I Never Dreamed
I never dreamed I'd have insomnia.

Love and Hate

I didn't think I could hate until I experienced war
After losing comrades I wanted to even the score

I think I felt love and hate at the same time
Or toggled so fast it felt like rhyme

Felt love for my brothers
Hate for those other mothers

The extreme was too much and too fast
My brain couldn't handle the emotional contrast

It May Have Been Purpose

I thought I had been seeking
Camaraderie for forty-five years
I searched for it in churches, clubs
Organizations and careers

It may not have been
Camaraderie I am learning
But instead it may have been
Purpose I was yearning
My Buddy Jimmy

My Buddy Jimmy

My buddy Jimmy was trained to kill
Today has that same mindset still

I've been the subject of his wrath
Don't want to go down that path

My job was to save lives
My mission was who survives

I even cared for both sides
Where compassion and revenge collides

Jimmy and I both have PTSD
Without many differences I can see

This disease will affect us all
No matter what trauma we recall

Every Breath I Took

I may not remember what I did yesterday
And I may not remember some words that I say

I may not remember your name
And I may not remember who won the big game

But almost fifty years after the war
I remember every wound I cared for

I remember every leaf I shook
I remember every breath I took

I guess the war impressed my young mind
There are some memories I can't leave behind

My PTSD Glasses

I get my eye glasses from the VA
I've gotten quite a few this way

I'm careful but they always get destroyed
It seems to be a practice I can't avoid

They always get these spots on the lens
Won't come off no matter how much I cleanse

I got some new ones just last week
Thick black rims I look like a geek

Had a PTSD episode yesterday
Put on quite a tearful display

Then suddenly another new spot stain appears
I realized then it must be coming from my tears

So if you see a guy with stained glasses you can bet
He's probably a PTSD Vietnam War Vet

Realized Today

Realized today...
I harbor resentment from the war
I'm resentful to the core

Realized today...
I'm resentful to our countries politicians
I'm resentful of my angry dispositions

Realized today...
I'm resentful to sit thru a group session
I'm resentful for all of this depression

Realized today...
I resent the general population
I resent our ungrateful nation

Realized today...
I'm resentful because my life is so uneventful
I'm resentful because I am so resentful

Welcome To My Mind

Welcome to my mind
Browse around if you're so inclined
You'll be lucky to find anybody home
My mind has a tendency to roam

Be careful if you open the amygdala door
That room is full of blood and gore
I hold those memories in reserve
It's my life they will preserve

Sometimes things get kind of crazy
My thoughts get mixed up and hazy
I'm supposed to have a mental disorder
Like some rowdy unwanted boarder

If you venture into the memory room
There's a lot to see I would assume
I've experienced a lot over the years
I've enjoyed many hobbies and careers

Some say I use only 10% of me
What a lie that turned out to be
I use all of my brain
I'd have to, to store all of my pain

23 vets a day put a gun to their head
I wish they would seek help instead
This disease must get pretty bad
23 a day is really pretty sad

Well I hope you enjoyed your tour
My PTSD has no cure
If you find a trick that will fix this
Visit again and we'll restore what's amiss

A Mental Workout

Writing PTSD poems
Is like going to the gym,
Except it's my mind
That stays in trim.

I Found The Cure For PTSD.

There are lots of therapies for PTSD.
So far none have worked for me.

There's counseling called one on one.
There's a group therapy that's run.

I've tried the Native American approach.
I've tried a professional executive coach.

I've tried eight different meds so far.
I work a lot on my hot rod car.

Started music therapy the other day.
Not sure yet what to say.

Every day I pray to God.
It even helps to drive my hot rod.

But I found a cure that makes me cocky.
It's called "Air Hockey".

Brain Ache

Everyone has experienced heart ache in their life
Maybe they lost a child or even a wife

Your heart can ache but it still keeps going
It continues to beat and the blood is still flowing

Sure the heart is important but it's just a muscle
It can't think, reason or resolve a tussle

Did you know that the brain can ache too
Emotional trauma can set it askew

When the brain aches it won't work well for long
It controls everything so lots of stuff can go wrong

It's easy to spot a brain that is broken
By the expression of pain that is so often spoken

(Inspired by: Jimmy Coley, Vietnam Veteran)

Thank you Grandpa Wayne

"Grandpa, I learned about the Vietnam War today.
A lot of our boys had to go away.

Bobby's grandpa flew a plane.
What did you do Grandpa Wayne?"

"I was a combat medic Sweetheart.
Caring for the wounded was my part."

"My teacher said you have a fire in your chest.
Sometimes you don't get much rest."

"I guess that's true.
It's funny how war can affect you."

"'Welcome home' is what my teacher told me to say.
And 'thank you' for the price that you pay."

"Someday you will understand this to be true.
My Sweetheart, I did it all for you."

High Stakes Counseling

Imagine counseling for PTSD
When you know there is no cure.
It's like entering a race
You will lose for sure

Knowing that 23 each day
Decide to end it all
The counseling stakes are high
When you start behind the eight ball

The Fear In My Doctors Eyes

I have seen the fear in their eyes
When they first realize
What I did during the war
And my issues we have yet to explore

One of my docs even backed away
I'm over my head, as if to say
So he referred me to another doc
I'm tossed around like a dirty old sock

I was referred to an in-patient facility
Do I really have that much instability
I wasn't admitted in though
They said I needed more time to grow

I was actually rejected
For the reason I should have been selected
That's like going to the doctor for a vaccine
And he says you're too sick to be seen

I wish I knew what my docs are thinking
When they stare at me without blinking
My PTSD must be rather severe
When they look at me with such fear

Invisible Scars

The worst thing you can do
to veterans with an invisible wound,
is to make them prove how sick they are.

Usually, it's a whole lot easier to have a visible scar.

PTSD Survival Kit

- Tissues
- Lots of psych pills
- Tissues
- Appointment book for VA doctors visits
- Tissues
- A long rope just in case they don't find a cure soon
- Have I mentioned tissues yet?

Boston Marathon Bombing

I just saw a news report about the Boston Marathon bombing trial. The theme of the piece was to validate the emotional trauma of the aid givers caused by the blast and the resulting injured and dead. The scene was described like this: People were down. People were screaming. People were bleeding. People were in pain. There was a helpless feeling among the caregivers with no supplies. Bystanders used clothing from nearby retail stores as tourniquets.

The news piece was convincing how such a horrific experience could cause such emotional trauma to the victims and to the people who gave aid during such a traumatic event.

I am very sorry this senseless event happened and I feel for the emotionally injured who assisted in the after event, but let me put this into perspective. Imagine that same scenario times 1000.

- What if it wasn't two people trying to kill you. It was 2000.

- What if it wasn't a home pressure cooker bomb It was a war bomb purpose designed for maximum kills

- What if it wasn't one single blast It was unrelenting blasts all day and night long

- What if it wasn't just one day It was every day of the year

- What if it wasn't three people dead in one day It was 300 in one day

- What if there was no retail store around for supplies It was 9,000 miles to the closest retail store

- What if there weren't hundreds of people there on site to help with the wounded and dead
  IT WAS ONLY YOU

I Need Predictability

I position myself in public because,
I need predictability.

I search my immediate area because,
I need predictability.

I'm sensitive to sudden loud noise because,
I need predictability.

I warn people, "no surprises" because,
I need predictability.

I don't watch TV because,
I need predictability.

I watch only G movies because,
I need predictability.

I'll write one more line only because,
I need predictability.

Silent Words Spoken

You can always spot a warrior who is broken,
By the voice of pain that is never spoken.

It's Difficult

It's difficult to speak of my pain,
because it's painful to speak of my difficulties.

Tears

My memories sometimes roll down my cheeks.

Happy Tears

Seems I shed many tears these days
My triggers fire in so many ways

I wipe my tears as soon as I can
It has something to do with being a man

I don't want anyone to see me like this
Don't want them to know that something's amiss

Rarely do I shed tears of joy
When I do, I feel like a little boy

I don't wipe those happy tears away
I keep them as long as they will stay

Homeless Man As PTSD Therapy

A homeless man approached me on the street.
He thought my hot rod was really neat.

I could tell he knew a little bit about cars.
At least he wasn't hanging out in bars.

He was very excited at what he saw.
Several times he dropped his jaw.

We had fun talking about my hot rod.
For ten minutes I lifted my facade.

It felt so good to have a PTSD break.
For a short time I didn't have to be a fake.

When he left, I gave him a hundred dollar bill.
For him it was quite a thrill.

He said "Thank you very much. I won't buy beer."
I said, "Don't worry about it. I'm the winner here."

That was expensive therapy at $600 an hour.
But worth every penny, to feel that healing power.

The 7 VA Rules By Which We Live

Rule #1: The VA doctors and staff are always right.

Rule #2: When the VA staff asks how you're doing, just grunt.

Rule #3: High-powered VA doctors will diagnose you, but a high school drop out will evaluate your claim.

Rule #4: The VA staff will receive a paycheck whether they assist you or not.

Rule #5: The VA staff doesn't have to be polite or respectful, because there is no competition.

Rule #6: If VA staff did answer a question, the answer is probably outdated by now.

Rule #7: If a doctor or the VA staff is wrong about anything, see Rule #1.

Uncomfortable Close

If I can hear your mortars
Going down the tube,
You are getting too close to me.

I Live In A Cave

When I was young and running
I built a big log home that was stunning

Now that I'm older and crazy
I live in a cave and emotions are hazy

Motel California

Since some dance to remember
And some dance to forget

Then I medicate to forget
Just like every Vietnam Vet

Veteran PTSD Prayer

Lord, grant me the strength
To accept the things I cannot change,
The courage to change the things
I can and the friends to post my bail
When I snap and go sideways.

Strategic Military Planning

The definition of strategic military planning is to build a VA clinic and PTSD counseling center directly under the final approach to a military air base where C-130's and jets are flying final approach at 300 feet overhead.

Rewired

My brain has been rewired they say
Not the man I was back in the day

Seems there's this amygdala section
That exists for my protection

All my junk is stored in there
It reminds me to beware

I'm different than I used to be
All because of this PTSD

Sometimes my circuits overload
My brain no longer meets code

I tried meds but they don't work
Sometimes I think I'm going berserk

Can't sleep much at night
I wake up in a fight

Is the amygdala vital for life
Let's remove it to avoid this strife

Don't want to trip the master breaker
That would mean I've met my maker

23 vets each day flip their master switch
Their circuits hit a major glitch

The Wall

Visited The Wall for the first time today
Walked it for a minute but couldn't stay

Realized it was built underground
And there were gooks standing all around

Ironic to visit the memorial of my war
Then hear the language of the enemy I abhor

This is my country and my war isn't it?
Having the enemy here is not a good fit

I didn't know quite what to expect
But I never dreamed I'd object

Feel The Steel

I could never comprehend it
How anyone could decide to quit
It's the ultimate of depression
And the final digression

There's always been another path
To avoid this deadly wrath
Until just the other day
When I was ready to die away

I could feel the steel
In my hand so real
My finger on the trigger
To pull it with vigor

I didn't have a gun on me
Or a rope to hang from a tree
But the desire was so real
I was ready to seal the deal

How could it go this far
My thoughts were so bizarre
I slept on it over night
And avoided that deadly plight

I added up everything wrong with me

Decided that was somebody I didn't want to be

It was no longer worth being alive

With my health taking such a dive

Acknowledgements

I'd like to thank my family for trying to understand me and accepting the consequences of my life along with me.

I would like to apologize to current family and prior family, the family before that and the family before that, for unresolved issues, things that I may have said or done during our short relationships. I am learning now that I didn't have a chance then. I am doing better now only because I live in a cave. I'm protecting myself from you and you from me. It's best this way.

For more books by this author, visit:
EaglesWingPublishing.com

To read more PTSD poetry by this author since the publishing of this book, visit:
VietnamWarPTSDPoems.com